THE
Best Gift
EVER

ISBN 978-1-0980-6118-0 (paperback)
ISBN 978-1-0980-6119-7 (digital)

Christian Faith Publishing, Inc.
832 Park Avenue
Meadville, PA 16335
www.christianfaithpublishing.com

Printed in the United States of America

THE Best Gift EVER

BEA KWOK

magine a very special place called HoneyComb Land. This is the place where TiTi Bee lives. Who is TiTi Bee, you might ask? Well, TiTi Bee is a super smart bee who buzzes around everywhere and teaches little kids (just like you) all about the stories in the Bible.

She travels back in time in her HoneyComb Time Machine so she can show everyone all the amazing things that God has done for us.

One Christmas Day, TiTi Bee was buzzing around and came across a little girl named Mandee. Mandee was crying and crying.

So TiTi Bee asked, "Mandee, why are you crying?"

Mandee replied, "I got all these gifts for Christmas, but none of them is what I really wanted!"

TiTi Bee said to Mandee, "Don't worry, let me take you back in my HoneyComb Time Machine, and I will show you that you've already received the best gift ever from God!"

In the HoneyComb Time Machine, TiTi Bee and Mandee traveled back to over two thousand years ago! As they look out the window of the HoneyComb Time Machine, they saw an angel and a young woman.

The angel's name was Gabriel, and the woman's name was Mary.

Gabriel, the angel, said to Mary, "Greetings, favored one! God is with you!"

Mary was so confused, but the angel said to her, "Do not be afraid, Mary. God has picked you to be the mother of his son! You will name him Jesus!"

TiTi Bee and Mandee followed Mary and her husband, Joseph, as they walked back to their hometown called Bethlehem.

Back in that time, the leader of Rome was Caesar Augustus. He told people to go back to their hometown so they can be counted and pay taxes to Rome.

When Mary and Joseph arrived in Bethlehem, the inns were full and there was no room for them to stay the night!

The innkeeper felt very bad that he had no place for Mary and Joseph to sleep! So he let them stay in the barn!

It was here in the barn where Jesus was born. Mary placed Jesus on a bed of hay in the manger.

This was the very first Christmas when God gave us his only son named Jesus—the best gift ever!

On this same night that Jesus was born, there were shepherds in the nearby fields who saw the sky light up with angels! The shepherds were scared, but the angels said to the shepherds, "Do not be afraid! We have good news for you! God's son was born!" The angels told the shepherds to go spread the good news that God has just given us the best gift ever— his son, Jesus!

The shepherds went to visit the barn where Jesus was born, and they found Jesus in the manger.

The shepherds said to Mary and Joseph, "We saw angels in the sky, and they told us all about the birth of Jesus! Glory be to God!"

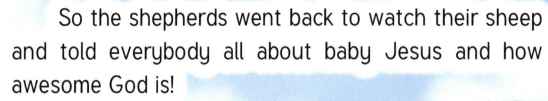

So the shepherds went back to watch their sheep and told everybody all about baby Jesus and how awesome God is!

TiTi Bee and Mandee traveled back home to HoneyComb Land in their HoneyComb Time Machine.

Mandee said, "TiTi Bee, thank you for showing me that story about how God gave us his son—the best gift ever! Let's celebrate together and sing the happy birthday song to Jesus!"

They sang, "Happy birthday to you! Happy birthday to you! Happy birthday, dear Jesus. Happy birthday to you!"

The End

About the Author

Bea Kwok is a certified child life specialist at Children's Specialized Hospital in New Brunswick, New Jersey. She earned her bachelor's degree in psychology from Rutgers University (New Brunswick, New Jersey) and her master's degree in educational psychology from Kean University (Union, New Jersey). Throughout the years, Bea has worked extensively with children from infancy to age twenty-one at the hospital as a child life specialist. At her home church, Liquid Church (Somerville, New Jersey), Bea has served as an early childhood instructor, special needs coordinator, and high school mentor. In 2019, Bea Kwok was featured in the career article of the November issue of *Focus on the Family's Brio Magazine*, a Christian magazine designed to inspire teen girls in their faith. Bea's big heart for children and teens has continuously allowed God to use her as an inspiration and role model for our younger generation.

CPSIA information can be obtained
at www.ICGtesting.com
Printed in the USA
BVHW022140290121
599159BV00022B/544

9 781098 061180